ENIGMA

Copyright © 2017 by Carolyn Smith
All rights reserved.
International Standard Book Number: **978-0-9904736-8-8**

Published By:

TEN G PUBLISHING, LLC
NEW YORK, NEW YORK

This book or parts thereof may not be reproduced in any form, stored in a retrieval system or transmitted in any form by any means, electronic, mechanical, photocopying, recording, or otherwise, without prior written permission of the publisher except as provided by United States Copyright Law.

Enigma Book Cover Design:

Lucid Bird Gallery
Corrinne Forrester
Saleem Clarke

Contact Information:
www.dreamwritenow.com
Email: dreamwnow@gmail.com
twitter: @writenowdream @dreamrox
D.W.N.

In Memoriam...

This book is in memory of my auntie whom I lost at 11:15am on Monday, June 18, 2007. She has left a legacy and memories that will always remain with me. I will never forget the woman who was more like the down-to-earth older sister I don't have. She exuded sexiness without lifting a finger; taught me how to walk with pride (and tried to get me to wear high heels because she said high heels were sexy). Growing up, my aunt tried to lift my self-esteem but that was a lot of work. Pearly, you tried to teach me how to dance but I still have two left feet!! I've gotten better but I still and can't do the electric slide ...well up to a certain point, hahaha. To this day whenever I hear "Upside Down" by Diana Ross, I remember when we were downtown Brooklyn on Fulton Street and it was blasting out of a record store in the 1980s. You sang your own version, "Upside down...round and round" and started smiling! I was 9 years old and I remember saying to myself, "Wow- Pearly's cool!" I smile now when I'm not crying.

Some of your last words to me were, "...If you could only see what I see girl....oooooooh!" We always ended our conversations with "I love you". That day you said, "You know I love you very much?" and I said, "I love you too". I didn't know that would be our last conversation ever. I really, really, really miss you Pearly! This has been very difficult for me. At times I want to grab my phone to share all the good things that have happened but then reality hits and I'm forced to remember that you're no longer here- physically. Thanks for visiting me in my dreams. You used to say, "Never dwell on the past because it only keeps you down." There are so many things I want to share- so many good friends of mine that I wished you met but I know that you are protecting me. Thank you for being such a positive influence in my life. I love and miss you very much!

ENIGMA

~~~~~~

On Sunday, May 10, 2009 I lost one of my best friends in the world. Christopher Mayhew and I grew up in church. He was two years older than me, so it's safe to say that Chris knew me before I was even born. He always made me laugh to the point where my stomach would hurt or I'd start to tear up- (and he told the best jokes when we should have been quiet in church). We called each other 'brother and sister' and he was the coolest friend! You tried to teach me how to tie a tie…that was in vain. There was the time you showed me how to tag my name in graffiti, the times when we tried to out roller skate each other at Hot Skates (my skills were on point when it came to skating backwards- you can't front). You were always over our house for dinner or just because and life back then was good.

You encouraged me to continue writing my very first soap-opera like play "The Very Odd but Wrong Family" and looked forward to reading the latest "episode" every other Sunday. When you and your family relocated to Florida in 1989, I didn't have my best friend around anymore; we wouldn't be sitting together at prayer or ministry meeting writing rhymes copying artists like Run DMC, MC Lyte, EPMD or Eric B. and Rakim. I knew however, at some point, we'd either run up the phone bill or eventually visit each other. A day doesn't go by that I'm not thinking of you! Miss and love you much Chris!

"*Enigma*" unapologetically ignites the senses to comprehend the aspect of maturation through love, lust, fear, intimacy, heartbreak, self-acceptance, empowerment, and hope. *Enigma* investigates the unrefined human attitude and induces thought: as one grows older, should he or she only adhere to what was instilled, or develop a process of understanding for himself or herself?

Carolyn Smith is an English adjunct, tutor, poet, spoken word artist, and author of *The Scrapbook: Spoken Word, Thoughts and Stories* (2007), *Big Bowl of Soup* (2013); contributing author in *Urban Mindscape: The Journey to Reality* (2015). She received a master of fine arts degree from Long Island University-Brooklyn. Carolyn has been featured in poetic anthologies and has years of experience as an educator and open mic coordinator.

Dedication...

This book is dedicated to my Mom because she has always encouraged me. She has always been one of my biggest supporters and although she knows that I love her to pieces, I thank her because when everyone else turned away from me she stood by me.

When others took pleasure in trying to discourage or discredit me, my mom stood beside me. She continues to be my source of strength and I am blessed. I know love because of my mother! Thanks so much Mommy for being the woman you are. Thanks for all the jokes, hilarious sayings...(even crazier Jamaican expressions), your strength and support.

Without questioning the contents in my first book, you took your copy to work and came home with orders! You took my book everywhere and proudly shared, "This is my daughter's book!" Those who know us say, "Oh my goodness you look just like your mom!" I would accept the compliment but inside I wished I looked like you- beautiful. Today I am my own kind of beautiful thanks to my momma. To say thank you isn't enough but I am so blessed to have you as my mom. I love you!

Table of Contents

1. Closeness of Him (Stanza 1)
2. Rainbow After the Rain
3. Overload pt 2
4. Sandy 2012: NYC
5. Closeness of Him (Stanza 2)
6. Gathered Together
7. Musical Interlude
8. U & I
9. Closeness of Him (Stanza 3)
10. Weep
11. Flashback
12. Joy
13. The Argument, 2010
14. River of Truth
15. Closure
16. "?"
17. Deception
18. Canvas
19. Obsession
20. The Heat

21. Frenzy
22. Blessings
23. Melancholy Jones
24. Rest in Peace (My Auntie Pearly)
25. Haiti: 2010
26. Love
27. For Chuck & Sheena
28. Unconditional Adoration
29. Assorted Mood Swings
30. Deception II
31. 360
32. Thank You Six...5
33. Measure (For President Obama 2008)
34. Passion Marks
35. Candles & Mmmm...
36. Abundance of Affection
37. Sensuality (Mink's Poetic Interlude)
38. Take It
39. The Passing of Time (In Memory of Greg Andrews)
40. Haiti Devastation (January, 2010)
41. Thoughts

42. Resolution

43. In Memory of Those We Lost in 2011

44. Sorrow

45. Dreams

46. Daily Life

47. Sensuality II (2 Poems in 1)

48. Strength

49. Shadow of Misery

50. That ONE

51. 8..5..6

52. Reality

53. Words

54. Sexiness

55. Midnight Passions

56. Love

57. Daddy's Blue Genes

58. My Friend, My Love

59. Circumference

60. Embrace

61. Encounter

62. Acceptance

63. Blow

64. Resolution II

65. Jinx's Love Affair (Prose)

66. The Secret

67. Ooooh!

68. Craze

69. My Reality

70. In Appreciation

71. Reflection Pool (My Mom)

72. 2012

73. Walk Away

74. Unrequited

75. Mink's Seduction Pt 1(Prose)

76. Boomerang Shenanigans

77. Daydreams

78. Daydreams II

79. Once II

80. Soul-Gasm

81. Rest Well Robin

82. Old School Memories

83. And Then This Happened

84. Eros

85. Saying Goodbye

86. Mirror, Myself

87. Mirror, Myself- The Truth

88. The One In Your Bed Might Not Be the One In Your Heart (Prose)

89. Broken Promise

90. Confessions of a Soulful Sinner Pt. 2

91. 1992: Dear Diary

92. My Brooklyn

93. Not a Dear John Letter (Prose)

94. Hard Fought Love: Maxine & Lloyd's Story (Prose)

95. Sensual Switch Up: Deidre & Khalil's Story (Prose)

96. The Victor

97. Wasted Wet Dream

98. Mathematics

ENIGMA

1.
The curve of his smile
lets me know it's okay
to converse with him
about any thing

it's the long embrace
kiss on my cheek that reminds me
he is my friend first-
one of my closest
I treasure the day everything changed.

ENIGMA

2.
Uncovering hidden meanings on Coltrane's vinyl
we kiss crossing 42nd & 5th Avenue
politick over chicken & broccoli
debate the plight of mankind-

An uprooted tree left by Sandy
[reminder]
discrepancies dissipate when we touch
make love to ideas

Watch the rain drench the ground
discuss our first encounter in between jokes
Hendrix serenades …

3.

Open up earth
welcome bodies dying in streets
open up earth
blood trails increasing
find a way to help one another instead of fighting
learn to embrace the unknown

Cries go unheard
their voices muted-
"revolution" is a 70s expression throwback
we're one
one race
huMAN
mankind doesn't understand
constant killing desensitizes humility and camaraderie

Who's right, who's wrong is irrelevant now
parents bury sons
children tearfully bid farewell to fathers
families lose members
the summer of sorrow continues
'melting pot' on the cusp of boiling over
but this is 2014

Many suffer in prime time
elected officials are MIA
water hoses and dogs - 1960s
water hoses and dogs- present day
"N---er go home!"- 1960s
the revolution will not be televised...
as it unfolds on tv

War and peace [beautiful lies]
distraction everywhere
as we grieve and question the validity of one's life
what are we not receiving?
what lies ahead? what lies beneath?
HUEmanity

ENIGMA

4.
Dear Journalists and Newscasters,

When you report on the devastation can you please include the five counties?
You know Kings, Richmond, Queens, Bronx and New York
...five Boroughs were affected
can you share with the world that many lives are forever changed and that no amount of money
can restore severed hearts?

Please share that there are families flanked with emotions after hearing a member or two were killed trying to save their lives?
Children were lost, parents were lost, co-workers are missing?
Homes are displaced, boats docked in Brooklyn's waters now found in Queens or Staten Island without a forwarding address?
Size 4T jackets floating nearby as bodies? [No floating devices]

No power, heat or hot water -
a frost is in the air...the climate begins to chill out
while many survive without overcoats
Can someone share that all five boroughs have been damaged and everyone needs help?
Can someone share the truth...

5.
Kisses: on neck, cheek and lips
hugs and
repeatedly whispering in my ear,
"Is this good to you?"
followed by, "Feeling alright?"
Waves of comfort flooded my inner being
he wouldn't let go!

ENIGMA

6.
Journey…
two souls align
exchange allegiance
converted into one- synchronizing
face impending storms

Declaration…
watch endearing hearts collectively
pledge trust and serenity
observe a soul kiss
witness this moment in time

7.
'A LoVe Supreme' permeates the atmosphere
sketch multiple positions entangling with mist

it disintegrates as Coltrane continues
to engulf their ears in foreplay

blues become moans unaware of echoes
Congo drums beat a slow jam of ecstasy

Sentences become sound
bodies clinch

countenances develop dreamy stares
hands clasp
silhouettes straddle

lovers disguise their souls with
enjoyment as the night air kisses the rain

ENIGMA

8.

we walked on stars gathering speeches and love notes
at its nucleus we kissed under naked oak trees blowing in
the breeze
harmonized symphonies along the pathway
words glided across parchment paper- today it crumbles

we once stood in a room of possibilities
gazed at the reflection called obscure
traditional canvases unleash the painter's thoughts
our pocket of strength diminished as the clock
taunts with ticks and tocks

held hands in our sleep-
crushed embers are stored under pillows
tears drench king sized sheets
rose petals bare thorns

9.
He's my friend first - I cherish that
constantly in my thoughts during the hiatus
Never forgot his birthday
wondered if he thought I was crazy …[He does lol]
'Would we ever speak again?' [We have to]

'Would he accept my apology?'…
we experienced too many things not to
Could we move on?
we can't walk away
I will always love his kind heart.

10.
Raindrops kiss the earth
thunder rolled… in the distance
flowers, letters and pictures covered the coffin
newborn son cried non-stop
mother wiped his tears first-
then dabbed the corners of hers
prayers were rendered, hymns wailed
the family gathered at the grave site-
she will be missed

11.
He speaks in my dreams
thoughts trace the outline of my smile
he whispers *I love you*…to my ghost
his body is behind mine as we speak minus attitudes

…

An older woman eavesdrops on the conversation
        he's lying about the indiscretion
I seek information from a tattered dollar bill-
                           it should have been quarters
every passing moment reminds me of pacifying truths-
                                     erotic
falsehoods
Snowcapped mountains only exist on a postcard
his loving imprint of tranquility   exits as a
flashback

12.
A toddler runs toward his parents for the first time
drool style kisses are placed on his mother's cheek
he turns to laugh as his father smiles

13.
He rips her letter in half
words dive off the paper
liquefies into a whirlpool

I
Love
You

She is engulfed by tears
he watches the news

ENIGMA

14.
She sits by the window observing a whale
her mind journeys to happier days
slabs of concrete was once a field of grass and trees
it is frigid…limbs have withered

He haunts her dreams
but she's comforted by songs
she tosses in the night to avoid danger
he calls her name

He raises his hand to wave- it becomes a sword
it slices her wrists and chest exposing veins and arteries
he places the other hand in his pocket pulling out lint
he blows the mound of lint into the air instantly becoming sleet

No longer visible she collapses to the ground
the water covers her head
she drowns unable to call for help

15.
The location was neutral
they agree to discuss the situation
bystanders look on in amazement
the couple begin to speak though nothing is said
invisible walls inhibit embraces

They yell at each other
this non-entertaining, cluttered lust affair
makes him walk away as she sits on the ground
he leaves his shoes

16.

Immature aggravation
not allowed to explore one's destiny
hiding true feelings
dialogues result in headaches
conversations result in conflict
uniqueness
yawn
disgust
conversations result in discord
give yourself permission to let go

17.

Boyfriend's back rests against hers while he snores
voluptuous women form a chorus line in his dreams-
he smiles
semi-erect he remembers ropes and bruises
gasping for air and unleashing his core
turned on to women/ turned out by older men

she opens up
he looks beyond her yearning eyes and sees curves
mocha-colored skin
he kisses her lips then whispers lies
he strokes her hair and smiles at his fantasy

Lady friend sleeps
he returns to consciousness and calls another name
she shifts- his eyes open
gently tugging against the sheets he reveals her peaceful
caramel covered body
in a trance like state he kisses her collarbone

ENIGMA

18.
if intimacy was artwork what would you see?
how would it feel?

paint the beat of my heart pounding to the rhythm of you
raspberry red, dark chocolate brown, golden sun rays
combine to represent movement

spread chocolate over my past
lick honey from my tongue
produce a landscape of passion and intensity

Jasmine candles flicker
Will Downing croons 'let's get personal tonight…'
blend with me

19.
Sketch moments in your mind
pierce my consciousness with desire
energize your touch with a smile
determine your motivation from my presence
absorb the moments stemming from my kisses
reflect on my intensity when you're away

20.
his tongue connected with her earlobe
hands strategically rest on the small of her back

eyes pierce his skin searching to locate that sweet spot
(-aka- the frenzy)
hands trace sensitive points on his body
now rests at his waist

transmit energetic harmony
kisses are like drops of dew
lips intricately touch his and lingers there
her tongue blazes his like an inferno

the mirror catches the act

21.
Adrenaline wrestles with mercury

words become mumbles
slow songs seduce love jams

poets cuddle with singers
rain converts velvety positions into fine art

indigo moans…
amethyst shouts

22.
Man embraces woman under a pink and orange sky
summertime breezes guide bubbles to an open lawn
a toddler's endearing smile
a spirit of God embodies flesh
mankind is truly blessed

23.

Negativity whispers:

'yeah baby utter the delightful song of hard work
share the episodes of crying yourself to sleep
days you wanted to be anyone but yourself
…end it now
be with me
come to me
…your true lover…
your destiny'

One's past may cause skeletal bones to appear
like lost keys suddenly surfacing

the past should not control the future
bury false hope, fear and pessimism
walk in the glow of the present

24.

In a dream she said,

'You are blessed with my gifts.
 Several will be known to you, others you must seek…
 if you search you will understand.'

I followed these instructions eagerly seeking my destiny
but along the way
I staggered,
fell and decided to give up

In numerous conversations Pearly said,
'You're talented girl manifest
what's in your heart'
In [what was] our final conversation my aunt said,

You've had it so hard,
you've stumbled- but you got up;
you've tried and tried but for some reason
you're not meeting your destiny
Ooooh, if you could only see what I see…
Don't give up!'

In the midst of loss I gained assurance from my angel
In the middle of fear I accepted love and understanding
I wonder is this part of what she saw?
I miss you

25.

Bloody rivers contains dismembered limbs
rest in peace
overcrowded streets of concrete, teeth, and fingernails all
on display
help me please- I don't need to be on television-
get…me…out!

tick, tock
can you help me brother
hidden by bones and bodies
fragmented chapters of souls are now divided…and
missing

in between hurricanes and mud slides I am ridiculed
I am flanked by fire, stereotypes and soil
despised by many…fought for sovereignty
first country of Independence…first to open Louisiana's
door
first…to open Latin's quarters

do they know that I am fighting? Do we not need air to
breathe?
Fighting for autonomy- do they see us?
Do we hear them?
Rise from the ashes of anguish
Take flight, stand strong

ENIGMA

26.
Electric cobalt signals placated his mind
memories of unbridled feelings resurfaced…
she was overwhelmed remembering their connection
dark highlights permeated her inner being…
discomfort abated as sweltering temperatures engulfed the room

Sweat drifted downward
two souls yearned for comfort craving harmonious sounds
he was consoled by familiarity
drained by her inner beauty
and remained listless

27.

A mother's love transcends all things sees and knows no boundaries
in the end, a mother's love for her children transcends all
her love is endless, limitless, selfless

It is all we know-
it's like kissing the face of the Most High here on earth
a mother's love empowers her children to succeed at all costs
it doesn't rob one of esteem 'cause in the end
her love makes us love...deeply
in the end she welcomes us home after the world has beaten us down
she communicates "I love you" without saying a word

In the end-
if she hurts
we hurt...
if she cries
our hearts break...
if she leaves us   -   we have a legacy...
but it stings

28.
Devoted mother sits with her agile sixteen month old under an oak tree
soothing breezes kiss his cheek… he smiles
strands of her hair rest on his forehead…he is comforted
looking at each other he gazes into her eyes
his fingers linger near her lips
drool slowly trails to his ear…he smiles again
she smiles as she blots it away

29.

Manipulated my feelings with the curves of your smile
daydreams of your past interludes dances with my
insecurity
you kiss me unresponsively
fragmented glass penetrates my eyes-
leaves a bloody trail of tears
walk away

Turned back to whisper,
"I'm sorry"
blew kisses on pieces of paper that no longer holds weight
leave me to fall asleep
closure revealed itself in the form of a broken olive branch

ENIGMA

30.

The artist sculpts atrocities unaware of her future
she sees him approaching the doorstep
he texts, "I love you" ending the chat

steel kisses are planted on the artist's cheek
he converses in his sleep…
tosses and nudges the artist
calls out names

his dreams take him to cellars with cuffs and restraints
his dreams entice him to reminisce
blond hair, green eyed vixens rumble with him in his sleep

vixen is not the artist
artificial roses and stuffed teddy bears mask the
commitment
grains of salt spell out   L-I-E-S

31.

The pen hides my reserved stares
my thoughts are transcribed into the atmosphere
his soft brown eyes try to pierce the skeletal structure of my nucleus
We shared stolen glances

I remember when we first met
sometimes people remain in your circle
other times they disappear
most times people leave
…but the ones who return are special
where will this lead?

32.

You made it possible to show compassion
you showed me how to receive it
give…expecting nothing in return
no regrets…

Thank you

33.

(Chanting) I saw, I saw…and I saw
I saw the ocean part its floor
the bow and stems of mighty ships swayed back and forth
in unison with the wind
(Humming)
and I saw shadows lying powerless rocking back and forth
hums/silence then hums/silence
silence…then whispers
silence…then whispers
"A sower went out…and as he sowed…
some fell along the path, and was trodden underfoot
the birds of the air devoured…some fell on the rock…
it withered away…no moisture
some fell among thorns and choked it
some fell into good soil…"
(Humming)

so they toiled the ground
toiled the earth
the waters: is where they rest
(the waters) they ran to the waters for safety
they ran trying to escape jeopardy…[real life]
dogs barked… they fled
my great grandfathers spoke of hope [in between murmurs]
the trees sang the blues [peculiar fruit]
nurtured the cotton fields while preserving unhealthy diets
they gathered at midnight devoid of passion

Bloody/filthy pathways contained spirituals and
underground passageways
ragged clothing clung to stiff corpses in the murky waters
a people in search of freedom hung in shame
a people in search of hope never packed a compass

ENIGMA

shadows accompanied many on the road to liberty swing
way down yonder-

coming forth to carry me to
the whispers   the prayers   the hopes   the prince

he is here

34.

Slide your tongue over my collarbone
gently stroke my thighs
place your hand on the small of my back
send signals all over

Creamy fingers make their way…there (shhh)
liquid essence marks a trail all over you
"mmmm"
glistening lips say, "Let's do this…"

35.

Paint the canvas with my heart
blend color to produce landscapes of beauty
lick caramel from my paintbrush
cum with intensity

Create with me
produce an unknown color
absorb the moment
sketch memories from your mind
as the chemistry intensifies

36.

He intricately places kisses on my lips
eyes pierce deeper locating what was hidden inside of me
His tongue communicates thoughts of desire
traces sensitive points on my body
Dew drops transform into a spirit of truth
turn…over…

37.

Mink wanted to make love in the rain as the water pulsated
against their skin
he wanted to move to the groove called "emotional flips"
she's turned inside out … her mind became a blank slate
made love in the rain
she said, "explore, until all of me …is all over you"

She licked his ear
he licked her fingers
tongues uncovered mysteries
Mink's hands wrapped his waist as he spoke to it

she talked back
he kissed …it
she kissed [it] back
he said, "explore"
she said, "continue"

His body was against hers as they stood by the window
he brought her to the edge…of the sill
she watched him plunge into a world of nowhere
broken down to their last molecule beads of sweat lodged
near his lips

Damp silhouettes linger near the windowpane
whispering lyrics from scratched vinyl
uhh…love…supreme…

38.
Tied hands/smacked behinds
hot oils/spicy dice/blindfold eyes
dare
me

use your senses
insides deeper/get on/play
bounce/ride/grab/switch
Tap

39.
Tears search for a resting place it cannot find
life transcends to a whisper
what was once considered a fact is now blurred
Angels prepare to welcome one more

40.

The rivers cannot contain fragmented bodies
heavens chokes on the stench
children severed into silence underneath concrete
dust beckons the babies to join them in eternity

Hospitals implode yielding its patients into the afterlife
prayers are delivered…though some appear unanswered
negative projections are unnecessary
we serve a mighty God…He doesn't need deputies or mind readers

Broken homes, displaced families/ Ground Zero [familiar scene]
nations abroad begin to send aid…[will they receive it?]
"Can you help me find…?"

First country of Independence cries for help
one cannot place a band-aid over a deep wound
from the ashes of despair/ the ashes of pain
the mystical phoenix will soar
the discarded will rise again

41.

Rain calms vexed deliberations
and soothes menacing accusations

fractured lives peruse the earth with
low expectations of achievement

blended souls collide on
cruise control on the road called
'purpose'

42.

A woman squints in a mirror and huffs
drowning in a sea of guilt he sees her but does not
acknowledge
she hangs an olive branch on their door but it diminishes
the blemished mirror is embedded with distrust
he planted a seed of anxiety questioning the future
he attempted to water the plant…should he?

43.

You will never be forgotten I'll see you on the other side
we'll share conversations in my dreams
I gaze at the water searching from your reflection
the ocean divides fiction from smiles
Streams of tears part one last time
raindrops kiss the passageway that separates life from
stillness

44.
Thunder rolled in the background
we didn't get to say, "Goodbye"
it's hard to comprehend… you're not here
you were loved like family
I wonder, did you even know?

45.
He smacked it once then moved back…and forth
smacked it again then grabbed her throat
still pounding and grunting
said, "you've got a phat…" and flipped her over

Crunch time [he grunted again]
she looked at him
he shouldn't enjoy himself but couldn't help it
…it felt good

She adjusted her head
sucking last remains
they spooned again
…
she woke up

46.

Long lost friends smile and then kiss
he says hello completing her meaning of appreciation
two lovers quarrel about the quality of air
another quarrel about empty cereal boxes
a fly hovers overhead
two men collapse on the floor

47.
Blistering temperatures rise
Get undressed
moist silhouettes move in silence
lie down
cobalt procreates with flames embers crumble
touch my neck
make love to me in silence
tongue in your ear
drums beat
get on top
feel the closeness of skin
kiss me
anticipate anxiety…enter
let go
silver and wetness merge onto my fingertips
release
do over

48.

Loss gains a true friend
it is nameless, boundless, strong
a mighty force is born with dignity
it comes forth from the earth
it is a spirit of light and a mantra of energy
it stands tall exhumed in pride
it is Man, woman, Life, truth

49.
Behind her stare is fear
she holds back from all who see
what does she cherish?
Her gaze cannot be traced
transformation is impossible
failed to prevent the tragedy in order to appear innovative
who will love her now?

Darkness is a stigma death that occurs at midnight
darkness is crippling
her silence is deadly
suicide engulfs her remains and flows through her veins
the syringe of life is empty and captivates her bloodstream

She took her last breath with a sedative of gloom
her ghost walks alone
her shadow will not leave footprints

50.
Not a resident but he is
drift back to the days of call waiting and snail mail
way before text messages OMG

His smile was minimal then but welcomed
his intonation was a southern drawl but I loved it
complemented by a calculated disposition

"America's scar"
[CMD]
plethora of friendly Carolina descendants
dusty crowns are hidden for safe keeping
He was born there
but we met in the [PA] sticks

51.

The forgotten American scar remains
a carcass of what was
unfamiliar with your rich past
curiosity abducted my attention
why are you treated unjustly?

Your haunting presence
skeletal row homes accompany vacant hallucinations
I am reminded of Meeropol's "Strange Fruit"
Billie's haunting rendition reminds me of your cobble-
stoned streets
(generations of troubled bones rest in peace atop your
streets)
the ultimate resting place of lost optimism

Numerous visits permitted me to capture
the essence of those discarded
my objective is an attempt to alter the masses' perception
…and awareness
amidst misfortune I found loving companions
geared with kindness and good manners
they were reared in *this* neglected city
[CMD]

~Salute~

52.

Smothering, lingering arms blend tortured souls
moonlight winks in approval
midnight strolls in
Past and present turmoil
sunlight around the bend
help on the horizon
prelude to a kiss

ENIGMA

53.

She lived in Pennsylvania where the darkest person wore a tan
her ancestry is the domicile of the Mercedes
blonde hair, azure colored eyes nicknamed Micki
she was my friend

We were eight years old when we met in the boonies every summer
she laughed at every thing I said
although I wasn't a comedian
she thought Brooklynites were destitute…
thought I was from the projects- my house was private though

Micki thought Brooklyn was
the distressed chocolate city and wanted to liberate me from turmoil…
She had questions - I didn't have the answers

She used the word *colored* one day on the way to the pool
said I should know
said…I was unusual because I didn't look like her
I never heard that word at home
said…she wasn't sure we could be friends because-
I asked her what that meant…who is colored?

Wide eyed Micki simply responded, "You"

54.

Take the very last breath the one before I scream
inhale
trust the movement…excessive movement
irrational actions
View the moment entangled in sheets
Power over you? I control this
you own the surrounding
Watch the pendulum wavers left…to right
amazing force
follow you to nirvana…blood flows

55.

The Isley Bros crooned,
"Don't say goodnight- it's time for love" but in my ear he said,
-Tell- me how you want it!

Luther's enticing tenor voice segued inside my mind
"I refuse to leave until I see the morning sun..."
we began to rock/ time became the voyeur
intensity blushed as two spirits blended soul colors into enjoyment
kissing my collarbone he said,
Tell me -how- you want it!

He begins to suck as time shuts its eyes
tell *me* how –you- want to remain inside the heat
touching and stroking until...
I kiss and lick until...
my tongue is allowed to find your hidden sweet spots

Opportunity cannot linger where it once controlled
it sees two lovers in the ocean of embrace and can't help but say,
"Damn!"
chance allowed two to create way after midnight
to let flesh remain on flesh
wrists tied
necks held
fingers sucked
until...
breathing becomes necessary

56.
They returned to her room after the movie
thoughts pounded inside her head
he wanted to stay/ he knew she was ready
although she said "No"
they woke up next morning in her bed

57.
He put a microphone in my hand at 3…
I inherited Daddy's love for music…and his dark blue eyes
our eyes are brown now
my affair with music increased
Daddy's DNA is southern country gospel
my insatiable musical expression varies

I sang my first song at three
'Sing properly…' Daddy sang the stanza again
'Ready? Twelve men went to spy in Caanan,
ten were bad and two were good'
Daddy's infamous, 'Sing properly' proceeded after
rearranged the song to sound like a jazz piece

At three years old we sang duets
now our conversations encompasses art
He put a pen in my hand at five…

58.
Sent kisses in the wind hoping
they left drops
of admiration on your lips;
doused the remains of old love letters
with an alluring
 fragrance as thoughts of you
revealed a seductive smile/
I released rose petal cinders
from my fingertips into the air and patiently waited
for them to reach its destination;
I asked God to bless them as
they traveled safely to your heart/
love is in the atmosphere…and this is only
the beginning.

ENIGMA

59.
I truly wasn't looking
found an old friend/
I smile when I think of you

60.
Step into love-
appreciate all that it has to give;
accept faults without acknowledging them on a daily basis
learn to give without looking to 'receive'
learn to stumble, fall then get up again.

61.

Meet me at 8pm
on the platform called 'Explore'
where dreams to mingle with dares
and desire embodies hope

62.
People bring different views
experiences and dreams into relationships
one is not 'better' than the other
it's simply another opportunity to
delve into undiscovered domains.

ENIGMA

63.
They went back to her place after dinner
thoughts of anticipated pleasure pounded inside her head
he wanted to stay
he knew she was ready
she said, 'No'
change…[your] mind
"We don't have to do *any* thing tonight"
change…[your] mind
They woke up the next morning in her bed

64.
At Dawn:

Almost lifeless as a tear glided down her cheek
he stopped to observe her reaction
he slammed the door as he exited

At Dusk:

He returned to an empty bed
he looked surprised as his countenance changed
he began reading the 'Dear John' letter

65.
Surrendering came easy simply because... he said it would be.

"Yeah, come check me before you go to work" Alan responded holding his cell phone closely to his ear. 'What time it is?' Jinx asked rubbing her eyes trying to focus on her alarm clock that read 4:30am. "Trust me- just come through" he continued as his tone changed from serious to subtle. "If you leave now you'll make it on time...I wanna do something" he said. *Really?* She thought.

**

His front door was unlocked. "Baby?" *This is how people end up on Eyewitness-damn-news*, "Baby where are you?" she asked stepping into the house. All the lights were off. She was about to run out when Coltrane and familiar noises from a previous interlude emitted from his bedroom. Jinx continued walking and upon entering, noticed that black-out curtains now covered his windows and the room was softly lit by two candles. The electric blue restraints were resting by the top of the headboard of his king-sized bed. *Hmmm he wasn't playing- it's about to be on and poppin'!*

"Take off those --- clothes!" *Get out of here, we're role-playing! She thought.* The clothes were left in a pile on the floor. She attempted to hop on to the bed when he yelled, "Did I say you could -- get off the bed!" She watched her boyfriend place the blindfold and feather on the bed and fit a mask over his head. "Get up on the bed... now!" He said. "Didn't I say come right over? You wasted an hour of my time ---now you're gonna pay...!"

66.
Under the silhouette of nighttime
she learned to tango in horror
innocence is replaced with apathy
whispers hovered above the window seat
willow trees swayed their branches in accord
words were spoken without a purpose
laughter was lost forever.

ENIGMA

67.
Then:
Witness the transformation
unwelcomed by others
eyes once pierced my soul:
searching
probing
digging
inside my veins

Now:
hands trace erogenous zones
they emit a sense of tranquility
he touches the nape of my neck
his tongue ignites a fiery blaze within

68.

The rain took center stage
wet kisses against restrained wrists
upstaged the downpour that evening
his tongue…was…fur-i-ous

*
*
*

Five fingers gently glided along the side of his thigh
the other five yanked a full head of locks
a series of kisses guided his hands to the small of her back
they moved in unison from the neck to the waist…
the precipitation envied their movement that night.

69.
…and in the end
love is the nucleus
between tears and smiles
true love grows even
stronger when the lovers
are physically away
from each other…

70.
giver of life- breath of life
cannot be defined by mere words
it is
boundless/endless/enduring

we're given one mother-one father
they are loaned to us and from them
we are educated…and [sculpted]
some never acknowledge…others cannot re[late]

to those that have brought joy into the lives
of others and their children
we say and give thanks.

71.
"I am the woman I am today because of you"

Strength and wisdom embodied in
a mighty woman of faith
I am partially her now

I didn't distinguish my likeness then

beauty
grace
intelligence
and uniqueness is She

My adored mother- my life.

72.
Welcome to a new day
a chance to articulate plans
discover possibilities
embrace love/exercise faith
implore help.

73.

Let go of my heart currently affixed to yours
…leave your kisses at the front door
by the sign that reads "Out of the Blue"
don't ask to be cuddled in my arms
don't expect me to smile
*

Leave me ruminating on past occasions
if you won't acknowledge me
make me question what went wrong
if you won't love me
*

I shouldn't anticipate hot oil massages
by candlelight…
the ones that led to [Ooooooooh!]
You shouldn't yearn for extra attention…there
we shouldn't be in each other's presence
only to have an argument moments later
*

Go strong or not at all

74.
Him:
How could I say that I care
without playing a game of truth or dare?
How can I bless you with knowledge
when you don't have a clue
that I have deep feelings for you?

Her:
I think about days past
the smile that once lit up your face
now doesn't last
What could have been
should have been
interest I'm losing fast

75.

Mink wandered through a dimly lit corridor wearing a navy and sky blue barely there, above-the-knee sundress with high heels/ she called out to him once but never received a response.

She bent over and began removing her shoe when immediately from the darkness she heard, "Leave them on…you look sexy"

She grabbed her chest, gasped and quickly squinted looking around.

She felt his presence behind her as Ian covered her eyes with a mask.

His lips caressed her neck, cheek and collarbone; he wrapped his arms around her waist, whispered, "You are very sexy" and licked her ear.

Mink was about to reply when she heard, "Shhhhhh" and felt his finger resting on her glossed lips. She licked his finger…timidly at first (or appearing so) and then slo…w….ly wrapped her tongue on two of his fingers. She stepped back and snuggled into him as his arms moved from her waist downward.

Shifting her hips in unison with him she chuckled and said, "You don't play fair." Ian asked her to turn around and leisurely kissed her. She outlined the shape of his lips with her tongue before searching for his.

Mink began to remove the mask when he said, "Not yet…"
He had other plans for his captivated other half.

76.

Kiss me once then lie
utter words you think I want to hear
share deceit over late night dinner
text instead of converse
conduct conversations with everyone
else but me/tell me lies...but you see
I'm no fool/you might have thought you
got away with it but it helped to seal my indifference

Kiss me a second time-pretend to show interest
pretend that we have things in common all the while
your dating card is full;
your shallow character slowly surfaced to the top
...slowly revealing motives/
unexpected ending uncovered a shaky and ambiguous
beginning
why pursue when you don't have a clue?

Listen to little boys trapped in adult bodies
who swear sex is more important than nurturing
relationships
choose numbers over worth...
hide behind hardwood 20th century fame-
whatever makes you feel important
pat yourself for hurting someone
didn't deserve it
karma is a vindictive mistress.

77.

It is difficult to achieve
expecting to be caught by the net of security?
My path is obstructed yet again

Want to share my love with you
need to be taken into your arms and
feel protected from the day's worries

…taste you
drink from me
gently suck on your neck
searching for the familiar spot

I want to share my thoughts…
the ones that keep me up half the night
ones that allow smiles
the ones that continuously imbalance the scale
I want to do all of these things…
it is hard to jump out

78.
Let's kiss before the wind caresses my thoughts
touch my tongue with a hint of exaggeration
open my imagination to endless possibilities
draw me closer to you

ENIGMA

79.
Imagine resting your head
on a comfortable pillow
kisses are placed on your
ears, neck and lips
a tongue traces your body
searching for a destination

Meanwhile
enjoy the ride of your life
reverse and forward
slowly then…a little faster
swaying back and forth in
between ooooh's and ohhhh's

Imagine ascending to
another level through emotions
rediscovering what
'once' all over again

80.

Touch my neck
lick my skin
ignite the fire
that lies between
our eyes~ and legs

Flick your tongue
over my collarbone
run your hands
on down my back
rest them on the
phat astronomical posterior
lingering there

Take me down
without saying a word
transfer hunger appearing
in your eyes to me
it's a treasure map waiting
to be discovered AGAIN

Kiss both lips and
…and linger there
tongue inside until
your throat floods
discover me over again
excite me all over again

Tilt your head backwards
as you linger there
until you say …until …
until …just linger there

Remain in the moment until
one tear traces down your cheek-
because you miss lingering here
don't stop until we fall asleep

81.
Some made us laugh for decades
we however don't know the pain
one feels and lives with behind the shades

Robin Williams took his own life
do we understand the turmoil
one must be fighting in order to end the strife?

Death by apparent asphyxia ...
We're going to miss ya
more importantly what was haunting you
that no one could see?

Black hole of depression..
the abyss hardly escaping on a daily basis
we must face this-
who are the people responsible
for helping celebs face their
fears, demons, past unknown?

Who will sing for the one that
has shown us brilliance
helped alleviate our pain...
but he couldn't gain control
of his nightmares...

Rest now.

82.

We met when sugar daddies were 5 cents
blue on grey suede Pumas sneakers had fat laces
(watch your patches) royal blue straight leg Lee jeans
looked fly with a customized T-shirt

his brown eyes penetrated the structure of my nucleus
trapped behind my words
the pen hid desires
[zodiac] Crabs are infectious

83.
informal thoughts/along with angst
romance on sizzle in the afternoon
conversations in between
[eating] subs and [drinking] water

city of love adored me…
kisses strategically placed here and there
conjured past feelings

yes? again? right now?

ivory sheets overwhelm liberated eyes

dominance
concentrate
let go
smiling faces journey to another level
connecting in between
a navigational system with its own rules
long time coming

84.

Sent kisses in the wind
hoping they left drops of admiration
on your soft lips;
doused the remains of old love letters
with an alluring fragrance
as thoughts of you reveal a seductive smile.

I released rose petal embers
from my fingertips
into the air of possibility
asking God to bless them
as they traveled safely to your heart.

Spanish Translation:
Envie besos el viento esperando que den gotas de
admiracion a tus labios suaves;
roce los restos de viejas cartas de amor en una fragrancia
seductora mientras pensamientos de ti revelaron una
sonrisa seductora.

Lanze petalos de rosas de mis dedos hacia el aire de
posibilidad pidiendo a Dios que los bendiga mientras
viajaban de manera segura a tu corazon.

ENIGMA

85.
walk away don't turn into a pillar of salt
don't go back but lack of confidence brought
compromise
dirty footprints also left trails of broken bottles in the sand

confessions of a soulful sinner...secrets taken
to the grave
"maybe if he sees"... the [beginning] sentence of disaster

time leaves angst and regret
if fortune cookies only told the truth...
if zodiac's compatibility was really accurate.

86.
face the light
smile of torment
silky words, empty promises
handsome performer- believer of self

deceiving conversations
sinister intentions
"what about me? don't you love me?"
uncontained ego

mumbling thoughts with myself over a cup of white mocha
chocolate
facing my fears for once
staring into the mirror
staring into the mirror of loneliness
confronted with past thoughts and
actions

guilt ridden dreams
interludes with regret and fear
facing them instead of running away

87.

He's not to blame
there's no shame
we meet many people in life-

who we decide to get to know better
is a reflection of ourselves

He's not to blame
won't point fingers 'cause it's on me
full house? crapped out..

raise your esteem
stand in your tallness

88.

They complemented each other so well… at least, that's what all their mutual friends believed. They were the 'perfect' pair. Jhann was beautiful, always smiled and was escorted to functions by her equally handsome mate Jameson. He always walked beside her- guiding her, [if you will] by placing his hand at the small of her back. They smiled at each other constantly. Finished each other's sentences- how could anyone not love them?

Behind closed doors however, the two barely spoke to each other. They slept on opposite sides of the bed. Jhann's dreams took her to happier times- when her life's love was Brian. She tossed in her sleep. Brian was the one that satisfied her trinity: mind, body and soul. He complemented her motivation by being just as challenging. He made her heart smile, made her think...the energy between them was a healthy balance. Explosive! She mumbled, "Brian" in her sleep once...not articulate enough for Jameson to make out the name (but it wasn't his name so he was curious about her dreams now).

Jameson bumped into her as he snuggled into his pillow ... she hated that he didn't sleep still! He was starting to irritate her even more when he tried to embrace her in his sleep. For months she couldn't figure it out. Jameson was next to her but Brian was in her: her bones, head, thoughts, her dreams...Brian consumed her being- Jameson occupied her bed.

ENIGMA

89.
I told myself I wouldn't go back
weakness caused the 360
the past reared its head
at the time I wore magenta colored frames

I remembered the laughs- had tunnel vision regarding tears
and ulcers
somehow I thought things would "be better"
the third merry-go-round

This time the carousel was problematic
never circled- not even once
this time tears filled wine bottles and soaked through
pillowcases
this time I imploded- health risks

It was always my fault- what I didn't do right
I owed $10.00 on a $2.99 purchase
something didn't add up...and yet, I stayed

Was that his fault or mine?
I hold myself responsible
the dullness of tarnished silver doesn't remove itself
it was there the entire time

False hopes
empty sentences
lying eyes
bottomless [selfish] heart
and yet again...I stayed

This was about my "place" in life
where I thought I was going
who I was going with
and yet in spite of lies and pain

I convinced myself that I needed 'him'
I was nothing without 'him'

I promised myself I wouldn't go back
my soul became a pillar of salt
I owe it an apology
the confessions of a soulful sinner continues

ENIGMA

90.
Alone with my thoughts
drifting back to a simpler time:
do you like me? yes, no, maybe

Awkward childhood to young woman
clinging to words instead of actions
stripping my dignity along the way
selling out for a backhanded compliment
or the chance to pass through life undetected

Never allowed myself to mature
stunted growth
beat myself up [do it before someone else does]
depression on hand [low self-esteem hangover]
lack of confidence
when will it end?

There's always a first:
first unhealthy attachment
one soul clinging to another-
there's always one

Never look back I said
never...well maybe just once
...twice
three times a fool

91.
Journal Entry:

his big brown eyes locked with mine
we stood under a huge oak tree
his lips were soft
his tongue deliberately searched for mine

hands gathered around me
he hugged and kissed me
nothing else mattered
New Year's Eve night...

in between each breath is 'hmmm'
a hum of positive reception arrests the midevening air

succession of kisses
intricately exchanged by friends
under the huge oak tree
during an unusually temperate
December 31st

backward and forward: connections to the past
linked my cheeks, lips and shoulder as one
he kissed my collarbone and the nape of my neck

92.
East Flatbush and Crown Heights
Brooklyn Heights and Bedford Stuyvessant
P.S. 91
penny candies and smiles
Rest in Peace Mrs. Raskin-
thank you for "Do Now" and "More to Do"
Madame Augonnet taught French -Bon jour!

Mrs Middleton and the rexograph machine
Mrs. Parrati watching over the mini building children-
we were and still are the Gifted and Talented
Mr R. Charles Rownd -sing or play your instrument …"U"-
Discovery and Ride On Band/ Beat It, Coconut Woman,
All Night Long
Fly's Up and Salugie/ Double Dutch and D.I.S.H. Choice
"Ms Lucy had a baby his name was tiny Tim she put him in the bathtub to see if he could swim…."
Ahhh playground games

Downtown Brooklyn and Cobble Hill
Canarsie and Park Slope
Roller skating at Empire
movies at the Kent or Rugby
walking to school

I.S. 391 Mahalia Jackson [not the complex]
watching the B12 beat the red light on Albany Avenue
fresh bagels on Flatlands Avenue
Roy Rogers up the street from South Shore
suede skirts from the Albee Square Mall

93.

I've been sitting here trying to formulate my thoughts into words and it's been hard. In trying to figure out my next move my gut feelings are still here. It's like pushing against a brick wall- it's not moving. My thoughts are not negative or fake.

This is not a "Dear John" letter- this is about me. Maybe it's not for anyone to give 100% to another human being.
Maybe we should give 100% to ourselves (in making himself or herself a better person). I know right now, I'm a mess- I don't have any thing and can't maintain and maybe you don't think about it …but I'm the one going through it so it motivated me to do better in searching.

I'm not projecting on you at all. Sex is beautiful ... yes it's very intense and very passionate --- but it's not enough. A foundation must be strong. This is weak- so weak it's imploding. Maybe I'm awake in a bad dream- running in slow motion. Maybe I shouldn't write anymore because it's starting not to make sense: you and me…not making sense.

It's time to end this fake ass Dear John letter because it's starting to sound real in my ears …real to me. So again this is getting thoughts out because I'm tired of them weighing me down. I suppressed them long enough and it was hurting ... I'd love to hear your thoughts but I'm prepared to not discuss it as well.

94.

Maxine's mind drifted to her love. They spoke the night before and she reflected on their relationship: extremely open and very intelligent...was it really? She loved their conversations...often sexy but always innovative. She drifted back to sleep with a smile appearing on her face. They would speak that afternoon but what started off as decent banter quickly detoured ... 'The argument that never happened' lasted forty-five minutes before the initial "goodbye" was said. Were her insecurities getting the best of her? Why would she allow him to win?

Did she really believe that all he saw was her financial status or was he able to see her for the woman she was and *love* her? Why was she so used to keeping people at length? Could that be rectified? Well first she had to call him back...

"We need to talk face-to-face," she thought. "It doesn't make sense to conduct this conversation on the phone- I need to see him in person" she thought. There was no need to argue and she didn't plan on it. Lloyd answered the phone and she began to talk...the argument began to resurface but quickly segued into banter. "We shouldn't fight- but we always do" she thought.

~To be Continued~

95.

"I wanna know what good love feels like- good love, good love..." Anita Baker crooned through Deidre's iPod speakers. Khalil was blindfolded, eating berries and whipped cream...

"You're feeding me berries in the morning?" he asked licking the cream from her fingers. "Tell me if you like what I'm doing," she said. Deidre fed him a few more berries and then pulled at his belt buckle. He smiled and said, "Oh it's like that?"

Luther Vandross who was next in the playlist sang, "I wanna love, wanna have, wanna hold you girl [so near] so make me a believer..." in the background as she smiled and responded, "I'd like to give you a massage...but can't do it with your clothes on," ...

Khalil removed his jeans, shorts, and T-shirt and asked, "Should I keep the blindfold on?"

"Yes...let me know if you like what I'm doing," Deidre answered. She pulled out a black feather out of her goodie bag and let it gently glide across his chest. He said it was ok and then said, "Let me find out!" She swirled it across his chest again and then placed it next to him. She let a few drops of oil find its way to his chest and began rubbing it into his skin. Khalil moaned slightly and said, "I like this!" She pulled out the blue furry restraints from her goodie bag and asked him if he'd let her cuff him to the iron embellished headboard...he nodded, 'Yes'. He laughed and said, "Gotta watch the quiet ones!" Deidre chuckled.

She said, "Do you know how long I've wanted to do this? You just don't know..." Deidre suppressed feelings for her friend for some time because in the back of her mind she wasn't sure if Khalil was digging her that way ... she wasn't sure if he'd look at her sideways for wanting to explore her sexuality with him. She wasn't sure if he'd understand that this was an extension of her feelings for him: the anticipation of simply not knowing what to expect, but enjoying the process. They were both pleasantly surprised. "I've been here, you could'a told me," he said relaxing into the massage.

She planned on giving him a full body massage...but he was now at attention. The music, the scented candles, his reaction, the oil...her thoughts ---

"How long can you go without touching me?" She asked.

Not giving him a chance to answer she straddled him. Khalil slightly lifted his head then moaned. He said, "Ohhh you feel so good!" She shifted her hips again and grinded against him until he said, "Ughhh" and rocked back and forth...he tried to free his hands to grab her waist but she purposely cuffed him to the headboard. The plan was to make him to feel the frenzy: wanting to touch someone badly... but can't. When she stuck her tongue in his ear he said, "Unlock the cuffs...you gotta...ohhhh shh..hh..!"

Deidre placed both hands on his chest, arched her back and sent him to another level...she felt the build up and screamed into the air! He was still blindfolded and moving back and forth ...and yanking his hands as if that would set him free... she said, "Not yet my love, not yet!"

96.
There's a chill in the air today
leaves descend and branches crackle in the distance
under pressure from footprints

She smiled at the leaves in appreciation
remembering the afternoon she loved herself-
the afternoon she vacated the dismal apartment...
and him.

ENIGMA

97.
He traded boxers for thongs and lace panties
He said, "You *have* to take care of me"
we existed on a lonely highway of thought- mine

Resentful individual
sleeping while walking
oblivious
shameful crimes of the heart-
limp away free man
closure is defined "f--- you"

Buried the relationship
under women, pride and selfishness
we became a ghost
why stay? why return again?
"This is about *me* not you"- echoes

Treading past haunts in murky waters
counterfeit ideas
fraudulent lovers
pseudo concept of self
who am I?
who was I?

"When will you see yourself for who you really are?"
don't let anyone sculpt you into their idea of a masterpiece
don't let anyone chip away your perception

Never waste an orgasm
don't drown in someone else's pool of hatred
avoid giving away your power
it's your love- your soul- it's yours
avoid residing on front street
you are worthy.

98.
2 argue
1 ends it all
1 points fingers
1 is the victim and falls

2 different sides of 1 highway
1 north
1 south
1 ulterior motive

1 open heart
1 scorned outlook
1 plus 2 equals ménage-a-trios

1 sun
1 eclipse
1 blood moon
1 vomits and moves on

1 remains stagnant
'Every woman will pay'
1 wonders where she went wrong
contemplates if she should've stayed...
[No]

2 can't agree
destruction and abduction of a consumed life
1 refuses to see

The Author Would Like to Thank…

I'm grateful to my parents who supplied me with pens, composition notebooks, typing paper, and typewriters while growing up. I'm grateful for my sister and relatives who make me laugh hard at times (and have become characters in my short stories haha).

Special thanks to Saleem and Corrine for a DOPE cover design! It's a beautiful thing to find people who can get in your head, understand your creativity, but are inspired to build on an original concept – and make it better! A million thanks!!

Special thanks to Nikki for listening to my idea concerning the revised book cover and coming up with a great idea! I'm still waiting on you to publish, but I won't say anything out loud (smile).

Special thanks to Alicia Pollock for translating a poem from English to Spanish for me!

Special thanks to my editor and good friend Ms. Lorinda Mouzon. Thank you so much for believing in my work and for your support throughout the years. You'll never know how much your words encouraged me! Can't wait for your next project!

Tanya Craig: There's never a time that I think back and not smile when I think of you. You looked out for me growing up especially in high school. You always encouraged me and made me laugh. I thank you so much for being who you are and thanks to your family (the entire family) for their love all these years! LOOOOOOOOOOOOVE you my sis from another family!

Nadine: My sistah from another family…Thank you so much for being in my corner. The beauty in true friendship stands the test of time and I truly thank you for that. It is a blessing to call you extended family girl! Love ya! (We're going to make it!)

Love to Merita, Kim Mills and Lea "Starr D"! Thank y'all for the laughs and support throughout the years- love you guys!

Special thanks and love to the following for embracing and accepting me as a part of the "family": Toufi, Marcel, Sophia: You all welcomed me into your homes and lives and I cannot express the love I have for all of you.

Tiffany Jackson: My childhood best friend since Kindergarten- what can I say? You have made me laugh and I'm so glad we're still in each other's lives all these years (smile)! Love you girl!!

Shelley and Joy: LOVE you two like good food!

Thanks to Shirley for making my transition to Philly so much easier. We hadn't seen each other in years but it felt like I saw you the day before. You have such a good heart and I am blessed to know you girl!

Thanks to the good folks and fellow poets I've met in Philadelphia, PA!

Mary and Zahra: Grad school was interesting for me. During my first year I was an introverted writer trying to establish my voice. My last year was exciting and full of fun because of the both of you! Thank you so much for the 'sistah-hood', all the talks, jokes, the road trips (raccoons, tigers and a damn deer), food, drinks, some more food and your genuine friendship. (Did I mention food?) Love y'all both! To: Omayra, Tejan, Sri Devi, and Tina -aka- the food crew: I enjoyed my years in graduate school because of y'all and have been humbled by your support and encouragement. CHEERS to more good times and laughs! Nique- I see you! Waiting on your next project girl!

Shouting out my CUNY John Jay College of Criminal Justice family: Remember the ice fights? (Alison started them y'all haha). Sending love to: Arturo, Tarik, Norman, Reggie, Mike, Nikki, Ondre, Andre, Laverne, Corey G, Sean King, Allison, Ron Goss, Eddie, Val, Big Kev (You know why I'm still laughing- please don't kill me), and Damion! Love you guys! Sleep in Peace Gregory Andrew (Greg and I met in high school and attended college together). You are greatly missed…such a beautiful spirit.

Cathyanne: My Looney Tunes partner-in-crime (People need to understand that it's healthy to laugh and the old school cartoons will make that happen- you're never too old to laugh!) Thanks for the long talks, listening ears, the encouraging scriptures and the stomach hurting laughs. You will never know how much this year alone strengthened our friendship- Love you!

Ines: My 'twin' sis from another family...I still crack up when I think of all the trouble we used to get into over nothing...you have a good heart! We had a lot of fun in the 90s and I'm blessed to have a friend like you. No matter what I know you'll listen, discern, advise and encourage. Thank you for that! I don't take y'all for granted at all. Thanks for the laughs, and just for being who you are. God bless and love you!

Monique: Ohhhhhhh Mmmmmm Geeeeeee – my "Pana-Pana" homegirl since high school! Thank you so much for being who you are, for looking out years ago when I was job hunting, for ALWAYS making me laugh and just being a good friend. You've said a lot over the years that resonated and I thank you for your crazy (in a good way) personality and kind spirit.

Corey [Grooms]: My brother from another family...(It is also a very small world). YOU were one of the coolest and deepest brothers I met in JJC and you still are. I know you remember sitting at the table chillin' (in between reading your magazine/newspaper and "observing" hahaha). I'm so glad we reconnected. I always look forward to talking to you (smile). Thank you for the jokes, poetry challenges, laughs, and for simply being a very good friend!

ENIGMA

Alo: Oh my gosh! Where do I begin Ma? (inside joke). We had some great times in and outside of John Jay. I'd like to thank you and your mom for your kindness and prayers. (Please give her a hug for me). Thank you for seriously making me laugh (especially when you start to rap *on the ground laughing hard*) Seriously though, thank you!

Special shout outs to Annie, Betty Bette, Joanne, Pauline, Davina Diva and Evette!

Professor John High: Professor, Professor, and Professor!!! You're such a blessing! The best thing I've ever done was take your class and met you. I will never forget how you introduced yourself to me at the Playwriting final and said that you enjoyed my play. Then the first day of class you greeted each of us with a smile and said, "Hello, I'm John High- welcome." To say that you have been an inspiration would be putting it mildly! I miss taking your classes but enjoy the emails. Thank you so much for all that you've done and will continue to do!

One love to the [527] Classon Ave, 115th, St Albans, Greenlawn friends who are my extended family. If I start to name names....too many families- but I love you all. Thanks to those who really supported and encouraged me throughout the years.

My MVBC & GC people: Oh man- you guys ... One love and God bless to everyone from New York City, Canada, New Jersey, Michigan, Maryland and Pennsylvania!

Denise: My partner in crime! You were the first person I met at MVBC who was down to earth. We had some craaaazy times up there. Your laugh is still insane and still causes me to laugh. The memories are ridiculous! We've had our ups and downs but the beautiful thing about time is truly that allows one to grow. I'm still growing. Thank you for one of the best friendships I have- "Brooklyn/Queens: Through it all, for LIFE". Love you girl!!

Terry: A chance encounter in the 1980s has brought us here. Maturation is a beautiful experience...I sincerely thank you for e-v-e-r-y-t-h-i-n-g: all the laughs, your listening ear, big heart (I always tell you that) and kindness. You of all people know that I can write up a storm but see, I kept it brief *ha ha ha*). You're the best T- love you!

Tiff: You were the first to tell me that the first book was available in Maryland and you were just as excited as I was! You have not changed since we met and were dorm mates. I will never forget the fun we had there and if it weren't for camp I wouldn't have met you. You know we talk about camp all the time and although we live miles away from each other, you are one of my genuine friends- love you!

Kenny H: Thank you so much for always being there! We might not see each other on a regular basis, but I never forgot when you used to visit us and even hang out with us in the city. Love you!

Sean R: I laugh when I reflect on the camp days and the jokes!!! OMG! Thank you for always making me laugh and for being a great friend! XL all day! Love ya dude!

ENIGMA

Terre: My fellow Aquarian sister, thank you so much for your kindness! You introduced me to the entire B-more crew back in 1985 and I am appreciative to this day. Years later we're back in touch but it feels like we've always been in contact. God bless you girl! Love you!

Joey: Memories are crazy (lol)…You still make me laugh hard and I am so proud of you and your accomplishments! I'm not even going to write about the memories…too many years but thank you for being a friend for real. Love you!

Greg J: "Gregree" You're one of the closest friends I have and I love you to pieces! Thank you for always being honest with me (big hug). Thanks so much for hanging in there with me, your crazy "I-need-a-moment *hand on my forehead*" friend. Thank you for all the laughs, jokes, all the times we hung out just to catch up and OMG, Love ya babes- you know how we roll!

Chuck: "Maaaaaaaaan lissen" I can't even begin, because I don't know where to start. Thank you for making it easy to share my craziest thoughts with you and laughs…do we laugh a lot and have a good time or what? I still can't believe you hit me with a snowball my birthday weekend, hahahahahaha! I still have your letters. You are a sweetie and I wish you the best in life- you deserve it. Love you boo cake!

Pilar: OMG sooooooo glad we reconnected!!! I am so proud of you and very thankful for your energy! God bless you and A Sweet Creation- keep on helping the youth girl! Love you girl.

Danielle: OMG I'm so glad we reconnected as well!!! You were a sweetie when we met and have not changed! God bless and love you!

We might not see each other on a daily basis, but when we do it's as if we're picking up from where we left off. The love is genuine and I respect you guys especially for your hospitality. One love to: Tickle, Jerry, Lema, Joyce, Pooh, Shannon, Sheena and Charlie.

Sunni: I still can't believe after all these years we've spoken on the phone but haven't met! I blame your brother (smile) Hopefully we will this year LOL, but you were always nice to me. Thank youuuuuu.

Reggie: We'll meet one day as well right? Lol. You're alright with me! Nice meeting you my fellow Aquarian (hugs). I remember our conversations- here's to giving back to the community!!

ENIGMA

Roc: I always sent a 'hello" your way...did you get them? Because we both know the "messenger" was and still is forgetful (LOL). Thank you for being so nice to me throughout the years!

Dave: OMG my dude!!! You always made me smile. What's good! Did you know who tell you I allllllllways asked for you? I hope so because I did (smile).

Bee & Marjory: I thank you both for your kindness! It was a pleasure meeting you both.

Special thanks to the graduate English Department of Long Island University- Brooklyn Campus. My opportunities have been flowing and I am forever blessed because of my professors, advisors, teachers, cohorts and mentors. My former professors, teachers and mentors- thank you, thank you, THANK you: Judith Gruber, Professor Lewis Warsh, Dr. Mary Hallet, Dr. Browne-Marshall, Mrs. Scott (RIP), Dr. Minta Spain, Mrs. Stopal, Mr. R. Charles Rownd, Ms. Nuddleman, Madame Augonnet, Mrs. Feldman, Mrs. Stanford, Professor P.J. Gibson, Dr. Kinsasha, Dr. Carol Allen, Dr. Renee Goodstein, Dr. James Adams, Dr. Timothy Houlihan and Professor Michael Blitz.

To my students from Long Island University- Brooklyn & CW Post Campuses, and DCCC: Thank you so much for teaching me, all the laughs, for working hard and encouraging words! My P.S. 91, I.S. 391 and South Shore High School people: Too many to name but I LOVE all of you.

Dear Iris (Israeli) Haas, I wasn't able to visit you since I graduated South Shore High School and I was stunned to hear of your passing. You weren't my English teacher but you were the best advisor to us senior president/vice presidents. I will never forget you! I'm sorry I never got a chance to see you. Rest in Peace Ms. Is!

Thank you, thank you, thank you Aunt Joyce Michel! You will never know the impact you had on my life. Thank you for your kindness! Love to the Michel, Scott, Douglass and Prophette families ~aka~ my former neighbors.

Love to all of my students past and present! You guys are the reason I continue to teach- thank you all so much for allowing me to share what I've learned with you! (We learned from each other). Special love to Ms. Juanita, Karina, Gloriann, Ms. Ana, Griselda, Daniella, Amanda, Nicholas, Maurice, Omar, Osiel, Fabricio, Ms. Barbara, Marianna, Olga, Sharmin, Raquel, Dianne.

ENIGMA

Last but certainly not least, from the bottom of my heart I'd like to thank y'all for supporting this project!

About the Author...

Welcome to my world! I have been imagining and creating characters, poems, lyrics, wannabe rhymes and songs since I was in elementary school. I was born and raised in a strict West Indian [Christian] household in Brooklyn, New York. My upbringing helped create characters and a perspective I believe people will find interesting and can relate to on some level. It will hopefully allow me to expose people to a world that will make them think twice when it comes to stereotyping or assuming.

One may think he or she "knows" me but unless that person was there, unless I let you in...he or she doesn't have a clue! I think the first book I learned to read was the Bible...I do know the first songs I ever sang were hymns, Little Marcy, country western songs, and contemporary Christian songs. My dad recorded our first "duet" together when I was 3 years old on a reel-to-reel. You can hear my dad and I singing ... and then my dad says, "Sing properly" because while he was singing the hymn I was scatting like a jazz singer! LOL! If I were to use one word to describe myself, 'enigma' is the most accurate because I truly cannot be labeled.

I am an Aquarian- we are a world of wonder! I wear my heart on my sleeve: if I love you then oh my goodness- you never have to question, 'does she love/like me?' because you'll know. My experiences, love of various cultures, quest for knowledge and entertainment helps me to develop characters people will be fond of (hopefully). My truth has allowed me to delve into subject matters worth exploring- therefore please prepare to be experience expressions of sensuality, sexuality, accountability, spirituality and transformation.

ENIGMA

My poetry, short stories, fiction novels, and future films are expressions of art. God has blessed with the ability to express myself through words and while much of my content may be considered 'secular', it is published because these experiences have shaped and molded me for better. I thank you for taking this journey with me. I hope you learn something and stay a while!

    Thanks y'all   ~ Carolyn Smith

Manufactured by Amazon.ca
Acheson, AB